Δ SANCTUARY

SANCTUARY

Δ KEN CATHERS

Thistledown Press Ltd.

Canadian Cataloguing in Publication Data

Cathers, Ken, 1951-
    Sanctuary

    Poems.
    ISBN 0-920633-89-7

I. Title.

PS8555.A854S3 1991   C811'.54   C91-097145-5
PR9199.3.C285S3 1991

Book design by Allan Forrie
Cover illustration by Kath Kornelsen Rutherford
Typeset by Thistledown Press Ltd.

Printed and Bound in Canada by
Hignell Printing Ltd., Winnipeg

Thistledown Press Ltd.
668 East Place
Saskatoon, Saskatchewan
S7J 2Z5

Acknowledgements:

Some of these poems have appeared previously in *Island, The Malahat Review, Prism international, West Coast Review, Tamarack Review, event, Repository, The Alchemist, Wot, Origins, Arc, Quarry, From an Island, True North/Down Under* and *Poetry Toronto*, as well as the anthologies *Whale Sound* and *Six Poets of B.C.*

The poem "Coal" was also produced as a poster by Pulp Press and was broadcast on CBC "Anthology."

This book has been produced with the financial assistance of The Canada Council and the Saskatchewan Arts Board.

for inge,
jason & devon

CONTENTS

thin boned thing
from the grey world
I grew out of

poised
in some dark
part of me

the sight of it
wheeling in atop
shore cedar

perched on the
sky. etched
image   remembered

from the first
shrill call   echoing
across these waters.

times he came home
on the short haul
stand out

had to show us
something he was
good at

way his face set
turning into the pit
away from us

pulling the wheel round
slow   hand over hand
his arms thick

in a shirt   sweat
stained   stinking of
sun   hot tar

(that was him)

other times he
snapped out of it
hated me
for baseball   striking
out   every game   cursed me
in the car   finally

after the season   for
not making him proud
drove home

sullen   & died next morning
nothing more said
between us

left a silence
my sons have
to live with

this door closed
between us
as I write this down

god   I can't begin
on what it's like
to hate you
          this way

my body is numb
with wanting you
some part to grab
          on to

& words won't do
writing this down
is only voodoo
          holding it

the poem   your image
& breaking
one fine line
          imagine

the pain   body
tensed on nothing
words   wanting it
          to happen

it is the sound
that moves
the dark water
around the deer
drinking, placing
one thin limb
deeper   toward
dim stream foliage

it is the way
words move
in sleep
through the music
of our breath
dreaming into
blood beat
language of
bodies —

live sound   trailed
through these trees
is what draws
me on   toward
the held image
of water falling
of deer   tensed
about to drink:
on the path   back
of the river
broken shells
where some night
thing   has fed.

reach deep into flesh
she told me
      the old woman

squat in the back of
a pick-up
      on saltspring

find motherblood, green
flesh, seastone.
      she is

a voice wrapped in
a ring of bone
      a horse blanket:

join up to a good
woman, get drunk
      get kids

your body knows if
you don't
      reach back to

something living
words won't take
      you there

to that place, old
woman, indian,
      her hand

reached out, blue bone
circle on
     my wrist

the touch of her
in the back of
     a pick-up

her drunk son driving
down a dirt road
     to the sea.

images in stone
made by a dead people.

shapes they remembered
themselves by

are caught in this camera;
animals etched in light.

movements, lines that
taught men living

glimmer on this film,
travel with me

in my own country:
memories I look back to

but can not know.

living by the sea
smelling it, hearing
it breathe I thought it
a kind of animal

& would rise
in the night
expecting to see it
hunched in darkness

like a whale,
black teeth tearing
the soft belly
of the moon.

tideless winter.
a few kickers lie
dormant   belly-up

paint-peeled on the
icy landing. off
shore   a loon thrashes

the water, splashes
the lagoon with crack
of shell-ice breaking.

turn around. there is
a face below the
grey surface, a force

in the dark shallows
waiting. hold to this
place. mark the way

tossed shells break
perfect ripples.
corrugated language.

listen. in the echo
there is something
to be heard.

words
do not come
through me now

there is
just this silence
I live in

under
the wild child
in the locked attic

this house
a dead end
street   where words

do not come
turn back
like birds

refusing to land.
myself   empty rooms
lights left on

gulls clustering:
the air thick
with their cries

& the stink
in the back
veranda   creeping

through skin   felt
like voices
echoed across

water. something
dead. fur seal
we found   two

days later in
the lagoon
below. eyes gone.

thing I was
told to stay
away from   but

couldn't. kept
coming back
to see the

intricate decay
way things are
held together;

fur slick   live
with flies   crabs
feeding at the throat.

& the stink
so bad we
finally towed
it to deep
water watched
the tide pull

this dead thing
down. its smell
part of me

now   even in
sleep   the carcass
surfacing

        my face   staring out

what is it
that draws me
to you

the memory
of your death
only a blur

an image   of
a man, drunk — falling
from the dark

pier, his face
part of the white
flash   dwindling

in the calm
water. is it
the sound, the

stir of the sea
against this shore,
the warm wind

that could be
a breath, a whisper?
I stand on

the same landing, a
gull cries in the far
night. this too

happened   as you died,
faded through the
closing retina of
water: you looked up
& there was
someone   standing

against the sky.
that night   I
was too young

to know you
though I woke
found myself

in a dark
house   calling
your name.

water-pocked   stone
sectioned by the
sea's run-off

we are
            calm tide-pool
            water   encrusted
            with shells

sea anemones
alive to some
unseen current

the way words
move in a
poem   or come

slowly   drunk
late at night   having
the weight of stone

marked by our teeth,
thick tongues, moving
to their own design

a kelp bed
swaying in the
tide   off-shore

a new syntax
we give into
or drown

& walking the tracks above
the harbour
I hear a lone whale call
through the morning,
call from the fog that is
heavy with salt,
the raw smell of clamflats
below.
through the fog, covering
transparent
as water, the whale calls,
makes the air
moan   again & again
with his song.

seagulls caw overhead
& through the fog
a lone whale bellows his
empty sound,
song I want to return
stumbling
this curved trainline one
tie to the next.

& the whale sounds   in the
distance   now,
moving out   through the sea,
calling with
the sound of water, sound that
moves through him;
his flesh moving this fog.
listen. it
is alive. this pale morning
I walk through.

lost, can't find you
on this dark road
rain   live
in the headlights

& there are eyes
in the night

something
by the road
leaps up
& stops

in the sickening
time slide
of tires

& I can't
shake it, all
over the shoulder

driving with the feel
of that crash
twisted in the bones

what if it's
back there
dying

what if it's
a kid hit
worse than
nightmare

not finding
anything on the road
though I looked

drove
up & down
for it

parked where
I thought
it happened
      & listened

in the dead night
to water

running
through the culvert
below

afraid
I'd found you
at last

hard to believe
I wrote
any of this

not recognizing
the images, lines
running on

past all breaks
of breath, pause
no sense

to the transitions
of phrase. there is
only one explanation

I have changed
completely   between
the writing & revision

cannot even guess
at what it was
once like
        to be me.

1   here is the poem
as given

or at least
part of it

the pieces I thought
something could be
    made of

as if they were
nothing before

2   in the beginning

        they were found
        in the shaft
        behind departure bay slope

            perfectly intact

        appeared brittle
        these 4 chinamen
        pressed against mine face

            like delicate yellow flowers

        waiting
        where they crouched
        down to die
        at least 50 years

            before this

        intent
        on the sound
        of digging

            that never came

3   & this
starting the same
    as the bible does

reminds me
of other failures
    trashed drafts
    before this one

the page wiped clean
to start over

knowing how much
had to be erased
    covered up

to even get back
close
to saying it
    like that
    straight out

in the beginning
was the word

4   nothing rescued
their names not even taken
for mine company records

extension, morden, northfield
company   where they were
finally denied employment

prone to lighting fires
in the mines
to heat their food
& asphyxiated the horses
the men if not careful

or set off coal gas
that flashed through
haulageways like dragons
collapsed cross-pieces

all this to cook
with the small enamel pots
the company gruel
    they were allowed
    to live on

5 writing this down
from draft

almost put mind
for mine

labyrinth of
darkness

places I could never
find again

or return from
if I did

6 they say this land is
honeycombed with mines

echoes go deep
return twisted
the way your hands

exist, moving
in time   to what
you're saying

knuckles broken
deformed by
the mines

going down
the first time
at age 12

& the coal
cut sheer, a
black sheen
    in the light

you never
quite got over
that

or the smell
down under
in the belly of earth

damp weight of air
heavy in the shaft
you never strayed
    too far into

the maze of tunnels
below, a dark web
sensed
    encircling this silence

7   incongruous
        the enamel pot
        found here

more like a
girl's toy
    in a doll's hand

the corpses held
in the appearance
of waiting, heads
tilted
    as if listening

not knowing
there would be
    no attempt
    at rescue

the labour cheap
readily available
    elsewhere

8 dreamt I found
a door
in the cellar
    opening on darkness

a hidden passage
leading under
lured me
    into this death

rattle of bones
strewn as I move
through them &

the smell of lair
there   in the
    earth chamber

& dreamt the cold
nuzzle of roots
    pulling at the throat

almost waking
to the touch
    the glint

of something there
in the dark
below
    recognized
    as it closes in

9 & this cavern
is too low
to stand in now

the slow jaws
of the earth
closing
    upon them

on eyes staring
eyes open
to stone
    darkness

glisten of eyes
in the dark mouth
turning
    to hold us

mesmerized
by those
openings

the eyes
turning to coal
    dust

on these words
I return with

echo of earth
closing
on their faces

    in my mind

10 knowing from the start
this would have to be
    dealt with

the corpses would have to be
touched, the illusion of dream
    broken

but what can be done
with that detail

the fact that the skin
fell off in patches

the hair shed
with the simple folding
    motion of collapse

knowing them long dead
it still made you jumpy

hand knocked against
coal suture
    in the dark

said you were afraid
to look, held vision
of flesh
    peeling to the bone

11   in the end
they were left
the shaft blasted shut
    behind them

houses built
over the digging
& the whole thing
    played down

not wanting
the real estate
    damaged

the story left
unverified

a seam collapsed
back there
    somewhere

& the whole lay
of the land
    changed

in a sudden shift
last whiff
of coal gas
rising

    on the night air
    departure bay slope
    november, 79

12 but the structure
notice the ending

strata of lines
breaking this down

the weight, pressure
of verbiage above

changes it

    lines down
    facts down

    names & faces filed
    back in the mind

    the poem
    crammed back

becomes black
becomes coal

    element of fire

fishhawk watching
from the dead cedar
        we look up at

caught in the river's
noise   we yell
into   our own echo

become part of
the downstream voice
that runs through us

& the fishhawk circles
turning on the wind
as it turns
        above the river
        in this poem

holding the pieces
of this day
together

that are to be
turned back
into words

& even the trout

gone upstream
        (real words
        in a poem
                of water)

cross in &
out of
        the white boundaries

hunting ground
the fishhawk
holds in his eye

at first it was bees
swarms clustering
        at the windows

but distant
untouched image
        on a screen

the next time
it was beetles
cockroaches
        inside now

the walls, floor
live with them.

this morning
my mouth is full
of wings

& of dreams I
remember nothing

do not recognize
this thing
        in the mirror
as anything
resembling
a face

1   trying to write this
for years   turning
the broken pieces

aligning words/
the shadow of sound
with this

image of you
I can't
    think clear of

2   the phrases   don't
look back
look back

there   saying it
if only I could
turn from
    these years

the shadow of you
there   in the sea
    beside me

3   the dream   old
worn with seeing it

you go down
you go down through

the cold clear element
& enter stone

become the image
of eyes

the river
look up
   with

4 place the stone
in the mouth
of the first caught

   so it will be
heavy with this place
& return

   so the ghost flesh
on the bare spine
will grow
   & not decay

   can't even remember
where I heard that
now

   but your voice
in my mind
keeps asking

   for the words   the mouth
to this river
closed against it

   why do you hold
back knowing
without you

   I can never return
will shadow you
always

5   the old words
come through, return
in dream

           time

past
everything remembered

geese go south
fish spawn

I turn the words
over   the years

there is a stone
on the beach
here

it is smooth
& heavy
       in my mouth

tastes like the sea
bitter   as your face
       returning

he is not there
the green man
I kept in cellophane
downstairs

gone haunting the streets
        the waterfront

moon   no shadow
on the road
he keeps to

already there have been sightings
        deaths

he is headed this way
out to avenge
his waiting
this fraud:

it seems we
stole from each other
        unsure of the syntax
            of who came first
            was invented
            by the other

you see I intended
to kill him
even went down
to his cage

found nothing
but the words
"he is not there"
traced in dust

lure of absence
felt beginning
in back of me

      doorslam ending
      of poems
      I am locked into

a cage of words
confining these days

HOTEL

1   this hotel
has been
our life together

sleeping each night
in a different room

beginning each morning
with a ritual
of broken mirrors
& smashed tables

wanting nothing
left   to draw
   us back

2   snow blowing in
the broken windows
of this
   the last room left

where I lay
you down on
a bed of snow

crease the night
with the fire
our bodies touch
   to each other

dream of a
demolition crew
discovering us here
   years later

the two of us
naked
frozen together
   in the sun.

3   even now
    the hotel does
    not feel empty

    all night
    the echo of
    footsteps
        pace the hall

    sirens thread
    our sleep   like
    a stranger's child
    crying in the dark.

    but it is
    the things left
    behind   that join us
    to the past:

    lost wallets, forgotten
    coats, a newspaper
    scattered on the
        floor.

    in one room
    the phone dangles
    off the hook
    waiting for the tenant

    who has just gone
    to fetch an
    ash-tray, answer
    the door

    & never come back.

4 & there are
no more rooms
to discover

we have turned
each secret panel
followed
    the inside passage

to the source.
there is no
way out.

we are held
inside this body
of dead rooms

watch   dogs
run free
on the streets
    below.

5 & each word
in this poem
a room in
an old hotel

made with
my own hands
furnished with
the flesh
    of these days.

to all those
who would
move through
these rooms

be forewarned
I lived in
this place &
was not happy

haunt this vacancy
like a draft
in a closed room.

6 I would like
to tell you
that bad luck
dogged us

that a famous
axe-murder
took place here
soon after opening

that the legionnaire's
disease was traced
to this source

but the fact is
this was low-
cost housing
to begin with:

floors buckled
windows fell out.
even the tenants
were despicable

kindled doorframes
for firewood
let livestock
graze in the lobby

(hallways littered
with feathers &
      bone)

I tell you
it was their fault
the Board of Health
condemned my castle

as a slaughterhouse
left nothing
but the carcass
of these rooms

to live through —
one day at a time.

7 hard light
the eyes
open to

nothing but
a partition
of cloud & rain

where the outside
wall   held out
the night.

this is our last
time together &
already I see

the wrecking ball
rise   dead as
a winter sun
above your shoulder.

if I was lost
in a maze
of streets & darkness

if I told you
I was, you would
think it only

another device
to draw you
near. but

these are details
rendered from
another text

obscure tongue
I've spent weeks
over, leafing through
    dictionaries, a
    dog-eared thesaurus

for the perfect word
duplicate image
of these dark streets

twisted lines of
a poem I have
become lost in

sure now there never
was an original
first draft
    to come back to.

I am translating
from scratch, dreams
drawn   half-remembered

into the pattern
of streets   these
words imitate

see too late
I'm caught
in my own trap

will never escape
these   dead words,
possessed by what-

ever it was
you searched for
down these endless streets

darkening with rain.

strange weather here
    believe me

when I say
odd showers
I mean frogs
cuttlefish

sometimes incredible
black larvae
pelting down
from a clear sky

I'm beginning
to think
    something's wrong here

have given up
explaining
small miracles

rats in the toilet
snakes in the tap

just pieces
that don't fit
this world
I thought
    I lived in

go ahead
name a reason

meteorites, geysers,
atmospheric inversion

it doesn't matter
anything is possible

this poem
could keep writing
into a lost
language

become
an animal
snuggling
in your hand

don't look up
waiting

by the time
you read this
everything could be
changed

a man
may have fallen
out of the sky
unnoticed

inventing this
small world
     with words

a few laws
of physics
     to allow change

it was fieldwork
in a white space
     I came to

variables of flesh
transient

black shapes
that moved through
     these findings

a process discovered
here
     I return with
     engendered
     in the flesh

COMING HOME

I hear you
at the back step

calling kids home
for supper

the echo of your voice
lingering
       down

the backstreets
of this town
       I grew up in

coming home   can't
you remember

I was always late
lost

a thousand miles
from your door

clothesline arcs
to the dead cedar
in the backyard

dance line of
longjohns &
lingerie

mime this wind
that moves
them

remember wanting
to be hollow
inside

to be
that free
turning

torso   hung
headless
          on the wind

taste of sun
on your arms
as you took me in

& I was heavy
against you, didn't
want down

hands cramped with cold
grasping
          for the wind
                    again

my father was a hard man
had little patience.

for swimming lesson #1
he dropped me off
the pier &

said now swim
ya bugger

& I did
trusting him always

though I could barely
kick free

of this burlap sack
I found around me

settling through darkness
into the cold flesh
      of the sea.

she is cool
as the earth
she works in

wedging up
the black divots
in the back garden

the way one sees
a woman   planting
a shrub   in winter

heeling the shovel
in, throwing the dirt
back; caught up

in the rhythm
of digging. it is all
she is aware of

no more than
ridding stray kittens
under a rose hedge

the small girl
thrown face down
in that dark place

held still
with the flat
of the shovel

& covered over.
how she shapes
the split

crust of earth
smooth with hands
soft as pastry

turns back calm
to the house
where she will

make tea, wait
for the morning
mail   tranquil

as this image
you create of her
remembering

the neighbour woman
who dug you up
the story of how

they found your mother
inside, changed
to the child

she was rid of:
one of your dolls
cradled to her breast.

at 3 devon
would close
tight hands

over his eyes
to make himself
invisible

& I would go
through the motions
of finding him

sweeping under tables
chairs, calling
into cupboards

thinking one day
he will close
his eyes

as I do now
to bring these
images back

sure those shadows
of himself that
went off to hide

haunt these rooms
forever   waiting
to be found

these are the houses
I live in
only in dream.

this one overlooks
a lake, another
has a private orchard
      a riding stable.

in each house
I am somehow
different.

my cars & children
vary, unsure of
details I slip
      out of character

am held in suspicion
by even my closest
associates.

there is something
of me, of these
places missing:

each house
an unfinished world
I wander by twilight

calling your name
to the darkness
like a child.

harmac pulp mill. '83

this is for the men
I work with

up before dawn
driving to the mill
they never really wanted
        to work in

mouths too thick
with sleep
        to talk

just a nod
to those they meet
by the gate
        at shift-change

& this is for
the men I work with

whose lives become
as much a part
of my landscape

as the smell of
sulphur & the
iron-mesh gratings

whose talk is
as harsh & continuous
as the machines
        in the workroom

running through
the lies, stories
bullshit   'til there is
nothing left
but the truth
about their payments
     fears
          diseases

sudden confessions
of theft   when
they were 14

     & lived in
     another country

& this is for
the men I work with

whose children grow
up to be disappointments
run away   forever

whose women
sleep around
while they work
     the night-shift

grow fat & ugly
& keep the house
as settlement

& this is for
the men
that I work with

who turn bitter
over insults
small or imagined

work silent
with ex-friends
for years

& this is for
the men who
cannot retire
      unbroken

who claim to know
nothing else & will
die a year later

this is for all
the men
brought together

by this machinery
that works us
      into it

who walk out
the same gate
each day
      together

& drive home
to our separate lives
      alone.